Freaky Phenomena

Grace Ramsey

I0891849

Rourke
Educational Media
rourkeeducationalmedia.com

Before, During, and After Reading Activities

Before Reading: Building Background Knowledge and Academic Vocabulary

"Before Reading' strategies activate prior knowledge and set a purpose for reading. Before reading a book, it is important to tap into what your child or students already know about the topic. This will help them develop their vocabulary and increase their reading comprehension.

Questions and activities to build background knowledge:

1. *Look at the cover of the book. What will this book be about?*
2. *What do you already know about the topic?*
3. *Let's study the Table of Contents. What will you learn about in the book's chapters?*
4. *What would you like to learn about this topic? Do you think you might learn about it from this book? Why or why not?*

Building Academic Vocabulary

Building academic vocabulary is critical to understanding subject content.
Assist your child or students to gain meaning of the following vocabulary words.

Content Area Vocabulary

Read the list. What do these words mean?

- *combustion*
- *phenomena*
- *photosynthesizes*
- *reincarnated*
- *savant*
- *semicircle*

During Reading: Writing Component

"During Reading" strategies help to make connections, monitor understanding, generate questions, and stay focused.

1. *While reading, write in your reading journal any questions you have or anything you do not understand.*
2. *After completing each chapter, write a summary of the chapter in your reading journal.*
3. *While reading, make connections with the text and write them in your reading journal.*
   a) Text to Self – What does this remind me of in my life? What were my feelings when I read this?
   b) Text to Text – What does this remind me of in another book I've read? How is this different from other books I've read?
   c) Text to World – What does this remind me of in the real world? Have I heard about this before? (News, current events, school, etc....)

After Reading: Comprehension and Extension Activity

"After Reading" strategies provide an opportunity to summarize, question, reflect, discuss, and respond to text. After reading the book, work on the following questions with your child or students to check their level of reading comprehension and content mastery.

1. What makes the *Mesodinium chamaeleon* different? *(Summarize)*
2. Why might people believe in spontaneous combustion? *(Infer)*
3. How can a headless chicken stay alive? *(Asking Questions)*
4. Have you ever witnessed something that could not easily be explained? What was it? *(Text to Self Connection)*

Extension Activity

Which phenomenon discussed in the book interested you most? Using books or the internet, research it further. What else can you find out about the subject or particular event? Write a story about a character who experiences the phenomenon.

Table of Contents

Strange Skies 4
Abnormal Animals 14
Puzzling People 20
Memory Game 30
Index 31
Show What You Know 31
Further Reading 31
About the Author 32

Strange Skies

Fish and frogs falling from the sky. A headless chicken walking and breathing. People bursting into flames. There are many accounts of freaky **phenomena** all over the world.

phenomena (fuh-NAH-muh-nuh): very remarkable or unusual things, occurrences, or events

Sky Sounds

People in Costa Rica say the sky hums. People in Canada say strange trumpet sounds shake their windows. Scientists say the spooky sounds are Earth's natural radio emissions.

Animal rain isn't common, but it does happen. Sometimes it's a rainy day. Sometimes the sky is clear when fish fall.

Forecast: Frogs

Frog rains are reported throughout history, from Missouri to Serbia. Scientists say tornadoes and waterspouts suck up the critters and scatter them. Eek!

One foggy day in Louisiana, in 1947, fish fell from the sky. Some hit people in the streets. Some landed on roofs.

Bird Droppings

This wasn't Louisiana's only strange rain. In 1896 and 1930, local and exotic birds fell for hours. The streets filled with feathers.

Unidentified flying objects (UFOs) are reported all over the world. In Texas, in 1951, a **semicircle** of lights flew above three college professors. Dozens of people took photos of the UFOs over the next few days.

semicircle (SEM-i-sur-kuhl): half of a circle

A Simple Explanation?

Experts reviewed the reports. They said the objects were birds reflecting light from the town's new street lamps.

U.S. military members saw lights fall from the sky into Rendlesham Forest in England. They claimed they found a lit, moving metal object among the trees. When the police came, they found damaged trees but no object.

Rendlesham Forest is a popular site for tourists interested in UFOs.

Abnormal Animals

Dogs jump to their deaths from Scotland's Overtoun Bridge. No one knows why. Some say something supernatural lures dogs to jump. Others say there's a strong smell dogs can't resist.

Suicidal Canines

Since the 1960s, hundreds of dogs have jumped from the bridge. More than 50 have died. Many survivors try to jump a second time.

Is it a plant? An animal? Both or neither? *Mesodinium chamaeleon* keeps scientists guessing. The microscopic mystery swims and eats plants like an animal. It also **photosynthesizes** like a plant.

photosynthesizes (foh-toh-SIN-thuh-sizes): turns carbon dioxide and water into food using the sun's energy

The organism is found in the waters around Scandinavia and North America.

A chicken once refused to become dinner. How? It lived after its head was cut off by a farmer! The farmer named him Miracle Mike.

One Lucky Chicken

The farmer fed Mike through his neck with an eye dropper. The plucky chicken lived for 18 months without a head!

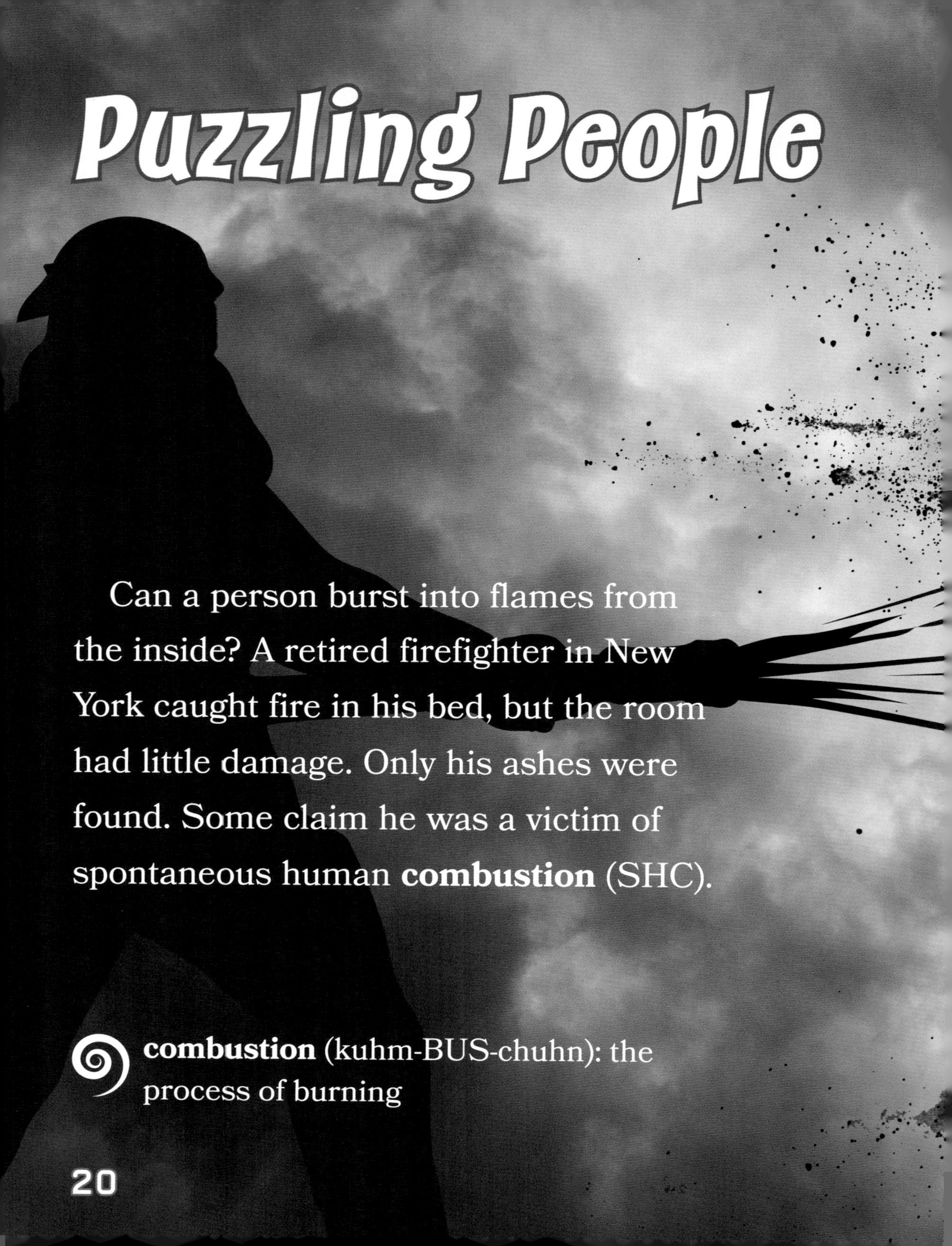

Puzzling People

Can a person burst into flames from the inside? A retired firefighter in New York caught fire in his bed, but the room had little damage. Only his ashes were found. Some claim he was a victim of spontaneous human **combustion** (SHC).

combustion (kuhm-BUS-chuhn): the process of burning

Is Spontaneous Human Combustion Real?

SHC hasn't been proven nor disproven. But most scientists don't think humans can catch fire on their own.

Dance fever may be real. And it may be contagious! Outbreaks of the dancing plague, or choreomania, have been reported all over the world. In one case, a group of children danced for 12 miles (19 kilometers).

Dancing Disaster

More than 200 people in Germany danced across a bridge in 1278. The bridge collapsed under the strain.

Some reports of choreomania claim hundreds of people danced for months.

Can you start a fire with your eyes? People say a young boy in Italy could. In 1982, Benedetto Supino was reading a comic book when it burst into flames. After that, fires often started around him.

BOOM

A brain injury can cause lasting damage. It can also cause accidental genius. Some people suddenly gain exceptional math skills. Others gain artistic skills such as painting or playing music.

savant (sah-VAHNT): person who exhibits exceptional skill or brilliance in a limited area

Acquired Savant Syndrome

One woman became a gifted poet and mathematician after a head injury. She sees sounds and hears colors. There are many documented cases of acquired **savant** syndrome.

Can a person be **reincarnated**? Thousands of children have claimed to remember a past life. They know things about people they've never met and places they've never been. Many cases involve a past life that ended violently.

reincarnated (ree-in-kahr-NAY-ted): born again in another body after dying

Strange Coincidence or Something More?

Some children with these memories have nightmares. They may have birthmarks that match wounds the person suffered.

Memory Game

Can you match the image to what you read?

Index

brain 26
choreomania 22
Mesodinium chamaeleon 16
Overtoun Bridge 14
past life 28
Rendlesham Forest 12, 13
Supino, Benedetto 24
unidentified flying objects (UFOs) 10, 13

Show What You Know

1. What is choreomania?
2. How did the farmer feed Mike the chicken?
3. What happened in Rendlesham Forest?
4. What is acquired savant syndrome?
5. What happens at Overtoun Bridge?

Further Reading

Allen, Judy, *Unexplained: An Encyclopedia of Curious Phenomena, Strange Superstitions, and Ancient Mysteries*, Kingfisher, 2006.

Doyle, Oliver, *Strange Mysteries of the Unexplained*, Scholastic, 2012.

Teacher Created Materials, *Unsolved! Mysterious Events*, Teacher Created Materials, 2012.

About the Author

Grace Ramsey loves to read about strange phenomena. When she's not reading or writing, you can find her taking long walks and exploring new places.

Meet The Author!
www.meetREMauthors.com

© 2019 Rourke Educational Media

All rights reserved. No part of this book may be reproduced or utilized in any form or by any means, electronic or mechanical including photocopying, recording, or by any information storage and retrieval system without permission in writing from the publisher.

www.rourkeeducationalmedia.com

PHOTO CREDITS: Cover, Pg 1 & 3 ©francescoch; Pg 3-32 ©baona; Pg 10 & 30 ©Rastan; Pg 19 & 30 ©passion4nature; Pg 23 & 30 ©suteishi; Pg 27 & 30 ©francescoch; Pg 29 & 30 ©ArtMarie; Pg 6 ©taviphoto, Pg 6 & 30 ©RomoloTavani; Pg 5, 7, 9, 11, 15, 19, 22, 27, 29 ©ulimi; Pg 4 ©ivansmuk; Pg 5 ©germi_p; Pg 7 ©GlobalP; Pg 8 ©Tevarak, ©Floortje; Pg 9 ©Andrew_Howe; Pg 12 ©gremlin; Pg 14 ©TorriPhoto, ©tamara_kulikova, Pg 16 ©baona, Pg 17 ©lukbar; Pg 18 ©antonellabozzini; Pg 21©Pattadis Walarput; Pg 28 ©Slavica; Pg 4, 10, 16, 20, 26 28 ©vectortatu

Edited by: Keli Sipperley
Cover and interior design by: Kathy Walsh

Library of Congress PCN Data

Freaky Phenomena / Grace Ramsey
(Unexplained)
ISBN 978-1-64369-038-4 (hard cover)
ISBN 978-1-64369-100-8 (soft cover)
ISBN 978-1-64369-185-5 (e-Book)
Library of Congress Control Number: 2018955878

Rourke Educational Media
Printed in the United States of America,
North Mankato, Minnesota